I Wonder Why

Mountains Have Snow on Top

and Other Questions About Mountains

Jackie Gaff

KING*f*ISHER

KINGFISHER
Kingfisher Publications Plc,
New Penderel House,
283–288 High Holborn,
London WC1V 7HZ
www.kingfisherpub.com

First published by Kingfisher Publications Plc 2001
10 9 8 7 6 5 4 3 2 1

ITR/1200/TIM/RNB/MA128

A CIP catalogue record for this book is available
from the British Library

ISBN 0 7534 0538 5

Series designer: David West Children's Books
Author: Jackie Gaff
Consultant: Keith Lye
Illustrations: James Field (SGA) 20t, 22–23, 24t;
Mike Lacey (SGA) 4, 8–9, 20b, 21t, 23b, 24–25,
26–27, 28b, 29, 30; Sean Milne 18–19; Liz
Sawyer (SGA) 16–17, 19b; Stephen
Sweet (SGA) 6–7, 8t; Mike
Taylor (SGA) 12–13; Ross
Walton (SGA) 5, 10–11,
14–15, 28–29, 30–31;
Peter Wilkes (SGA) all
cartoons.

Printed in China

CONTENTS

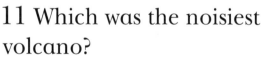

What's the difference between a mountain and a hill?

Mountains are larger than hills, and mountainsides are often steep and tough to climb – unlike a hill's gentle slopes. Some experts say that if a peak is more than 600 metres higher than the surrounding land, then it is a mountain. Any less and it is a hill.

● A molehill is a tiny pile of soil which, like a mountain, rises steeply above the surrounding land.

● About a quarter of all land on Earth is mountainous.

- A row of mountains is called a range.

Can spacecraft measure mountains?

Radar equipment is used to measure mountains by bouncing sound signals off the ground. Machines record the time the signals take to bounce back, then use this to work out how high the mountain is. The radar is carried on board high-flying aeroplanes and space satellites.

- The top of a mountain is called its peak or summit.

- Even though a mountain may be a long way from the sea, its height is worked out as the distance above the sea's surface – sea level.

5

Where is the world's highest mountain?

The highest place in the whole world is at the top of Mount Everest. This vast mountain is in the Himalayan ranges of central Asia, and it rises to 8,848 metres above sea level.

NORTH AMERICA

Alaska Range

Rocky Mountains

Appalachians

Sierra Nevada

ATLANTIC OCEAN

SOUTH AMERICA

Andes

● Although only 4,205 metres of Mauna Kea stick up above sea level, this Hawaiian mountain is even taller than Everest. From its base on the ocean floor to its peak, Mauna Kea is an amazing 10,203 metres.

● The world's longest mountain range on land is the Andes, in South America, at about 7,200 kilometres long.

Famous mountains

1 McKinley 6,194 m

2 Logan 5,951 m

3 Whitney 4,418 m

4 Popocatépetl 5,452 m

5 Cotopaxi 5,897 m

6 Aconcagua 6,959 m

7 Kilimanjaro 5,895 m

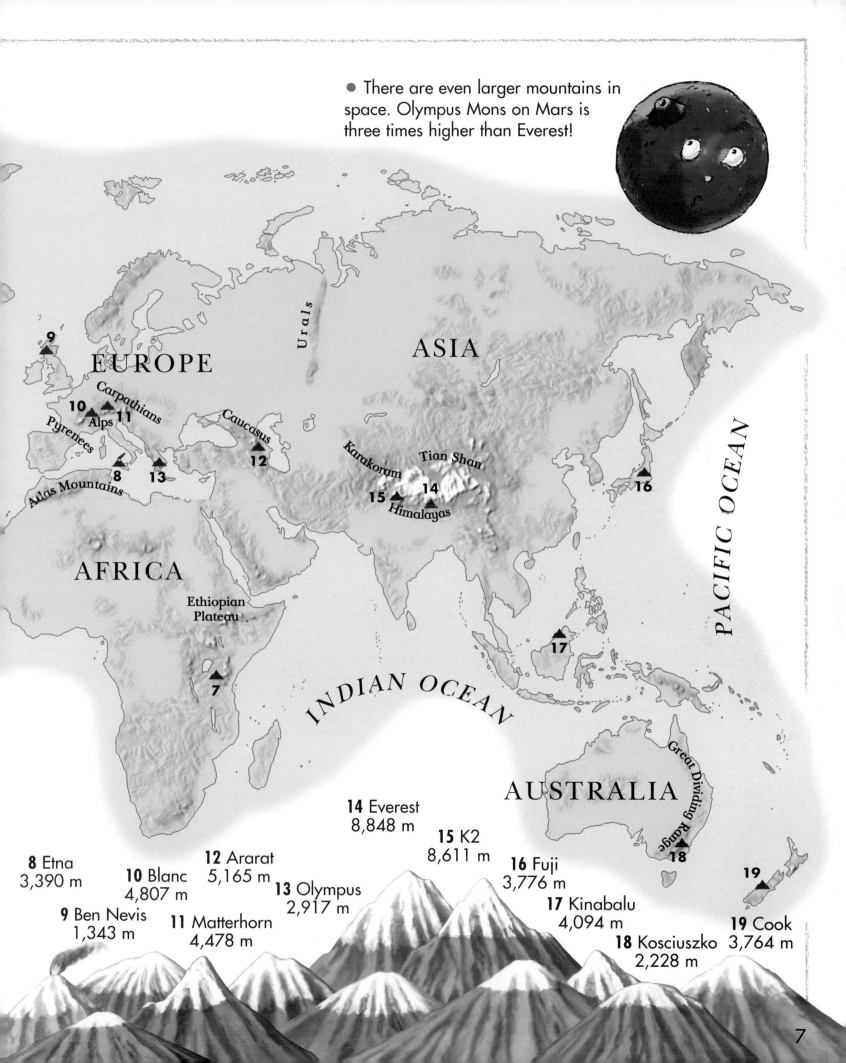

● There are even larger mountains in space. Olympus Mons on Mars is three times higher than Everest!

EUROPE

ASIA

AFRICA

AUSTRALIA

PACIFIC OCEAN

INDIAN OCEAN

Urals

Carpathians

Caucasus

Pyrenees

Alps

Atlas Mountains

Karakoram

Tian Shan

Himalayas

Ethiopian Plateau

Great Dividing Range

8 Etna
3,390 m

9 Ben Nevis
1,343 m

10 Blanc
4,807 m

11 Matterhorn
4,478 m

12 Ararat
5,165 m

13 Olympus
2,917 m

14 Everest
8,848 m

15 K2
8,611 m

16 Fuji
3,776 m

17 Kinabalu
4,094 m

18 Kosciuszko
2,228 m

19 Cook 3,764 m

Do mountains move?

They certainly do! Earth is a bit like a giant, round egg, with a shell called the crust, then a layer called the mantle, and a core in the middle. The crust is cracked, like an eggshell made from 30 or so gigantic pieces called plates. The plates float about very slowly on top of the mantle, because it's partly melted, like treacle.

Crust

Mantle

Core

● The plates that carry North America and Europe are floating apart by about 4 centimetres each year.

How do mountains form?

Although the plates that make up the Earth's crust move incredibly slowly, their movements are powerful enough to make mountains. Different movements give birth to the three main kinds of mountain – volcanic, block and fold.

● Volcanoes are openings in the crust where fiery clouds of hot ash, gas and red-hot runny rock called lava spit out. Most volcanic mountains form as lava and ash and cool into layer upon layer of solid rock.

Why do some mountains have pointed tops?

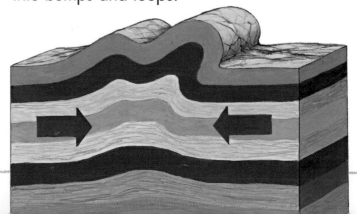

Even while a mountain is forming, the weather, ice and running water start to wear it away and carve its top into sharp points. The wearing away is called erosion.

● Wind carries grit and sand which work like sandpaper, slowly rubbing rocks away.

● Block mountains form when part of the crust is squeezed up between two cracks called faults.

● Fold mountains form as two plates slowly crunch into each other, pushing the crust up into bumps and loops.

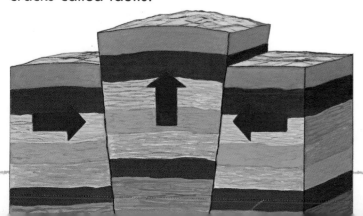

9

Why do volcanoes blow their tops?

A volcano begins deep inside the Earth as bubbles of gas and liquid rock called magma. This mixture slowly rises because it is lighter than the solid rock around it. As it pushes its way up, it gets squashed and squeezed. The pressure builds up and up, until the gas and magma explode through a weak place in the Earth's crust – making the volcano erupt and blow its top.

● The effect of gas and magma erupting from a volcano is a bit like what happens when you shake a fizzy drinks bottle and then take off the cap.

● When magma hits the surface, it is called lava.

Are all volcanoes dangerous?

● The ancient Romans believed a god of fire lived beneath a volcanic island off the Italian coast. They called the god Vulcanus – and that's where our word volcano comes from.

There are three main kinds of volcano, and they can all be dangerous. Active volcanoes erupt fairly often. Dormant volcanoes sleep quietly for years but erupt every now and again. Extinct volcanoes have stopped erupting and are unlikely to erupt again – if we're very lucky!

● Sometimes magma and gases explode through side tunnels called vents.

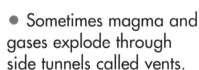

Which was the noisiest volcano?

When Indonesia's Krakatoa blew its top in 1883, the roar of the explosion was heard more than an eighth of the way around the world – as far away as Sri Lanka, the Philippines and central Australia.

Which mountains grow into islands?

There are thousands of tiny islands dotted through the world's oceans, and most of them were made by volcanoes slowly growing up from the ocean floor.

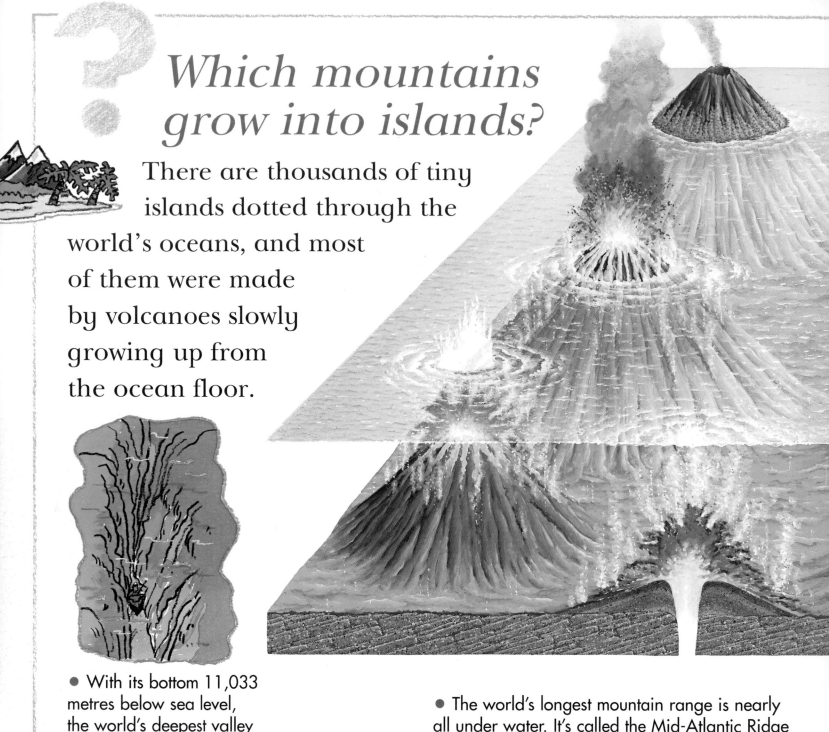

● With its bottom 11,033 metres below sea level, the world's deepest valley is the Mariana Trench in the Pacific Ocean.

● The world's longest mountain range is nearly all under water. It's called the Mid-Atlantic Ridge and it stretches for about 16,000 kilometres, from Iceland almost to Antarctica.

Mid-Atlantic Ridge

NORTH AMERICA

EUROPE

SOUTH AMERICA

AFRICA

ATLANTIC OCEAN

Can mountains sink?

Yes – an atoll is a ring-shaped island which can form around the rim of a sunken volcano. The atoll is made from limestone, and the limestone is made by tiny sea creatures called coral polyps.

- The water in the middle of a coral atoll is called a lagoon.

Lagoon

Coral atoll

What are black smokers?

Black smokers are strange chimney stacks that build up on the ocean floor and belch out steamy black clouds of boiling hot water. All kinds of weird and wonderful animals live near them, including red-and-white worms as long as cars.

Why do mountains have snow on top?

Not all mountains have snow on top, only the highest ones. That's because when water gets very cold, it freezes and turns into snow or ice – and the higher you go up a mountain, the colder it gets. The place where a mountain begins to be covered in snow is called the snowline.

● The higher you go up a mountain, the windier it gets. Winds can howl at over 300 km/h at the top of the Himalayas.

● For every 300 metres you climb up a mountain, the temperature drops by about 2°C.

When does snow move as fast as a racing car?

Sometimes on high mountains, a mass of snow will suddenly slip and begin to slide downhill. This is an avalanche. The worst avalanches hurtle downwards like racing cars, at more than 160 km/h.

Can snow move mountains?

Snow and ice can crack and break rocks, slowly wearing away the mountains. The most powerful mountain-movers are glaciers. These massive blocks of ice, snow and rock form high in the mountains and flow downhill like vast frozen rivers, carving out valleys.

● Glaciers carve out U-shaped valleys. V-shaped valleys are formed by rivers.

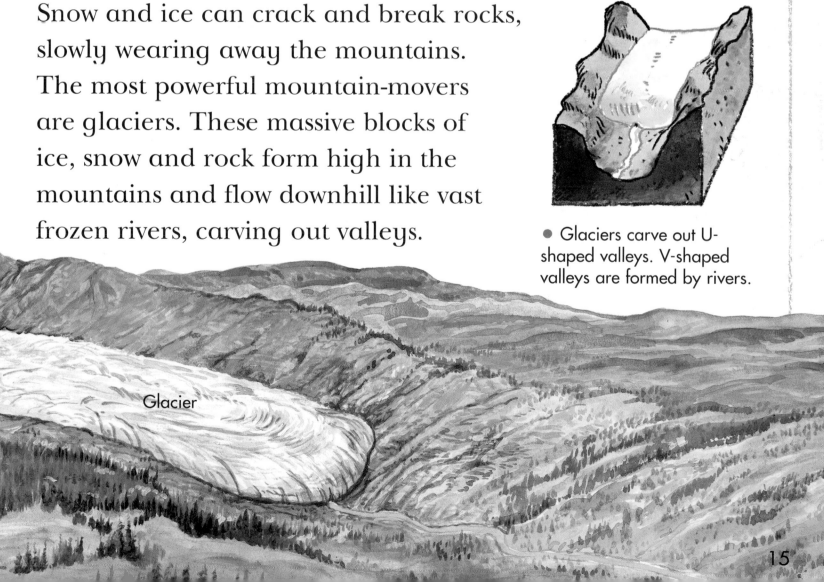

Glacier

Why don't plants grow on mountain tops?

The top of a high mountain is one of the coldest, windiest places on Earth, and plants hate it. Plants need water, sunlight, and soil they can get their roots into. Take these things away, and plants give up and die.

● Rivers and melting snow wash soil down off mountain tops, so the higher you go the thinner the soil is.

Which plants grow on mountain sides?

Large trees can't survive up towards the snowline, but alpines are small, ground-hugging plants that have developed ways of beating the poor soil and bad weather.

● The world's oldest-known tree lives in the White Mountains of California, USA. It's a bristlecone pine and it's already had 4,700 birthdays!

How do mountain plants keep warm?

Some alpine plants such as edelweiss have hairy leaves that work like an animal's furry coat to keep them warm. Others such as gentians have very dark leaves and flowers, because dark colours attract more of the Sun's warmth than light ones do.

● Plants can't take in water if it is frozen as ice or snow.

● The toughest kinds of tree are conifers such as pine trees, but even they cannot grow on high slopes.

Which plant can melt snow?

Like many plants, the alpine snowbell disappears underground in the winter. When new shoots start to push up through the snow in spring, they give off enough heat to melt their way through.

Can animals live on mountains?

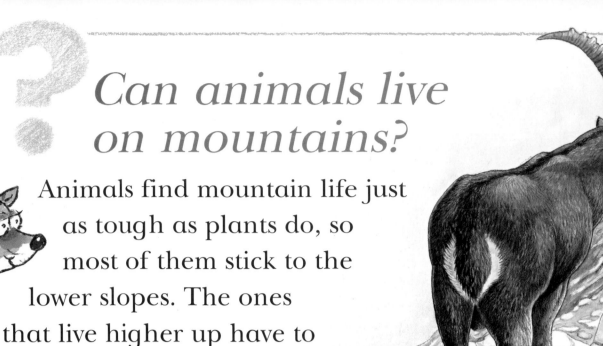

Animals find mountain life just as tough as plants do, so most of them stick to the lower slopes. The ones that live higher up have to be good climbers – like mountain sheep, goats and antelopes.

● The Rocky Mountain goat can climb the steepest cliffs. Hollows under its hooves stick on the rock like suction cups to stop it slipping.

Which mountain animal has a skirt?

The yak's long, silky hair falls into a skirt around its knees, keeping it warm. This is just as well, as it lives in the highest region in the world – Tibet in Asia.

How high do birds nest?

Although many birds make flying visits, very few nest high in the mountains. The record-holder is the alpine chough, which nests as high on the slopes as 7,000 metres.

● The Andean condor spends its days soaring above the Andes Mountains of South America. Its wings are wide enough for a car to park on!

Which animal became famous for mountain rescues?

● Some people believe that big, hairy, apelike creatures called yetis live in the Himalayas. However, no one has ever proved that yetis really exist.

Saint Bernards are big, clever dogs that are famous for rescuing travellers who lose their way in snowy mountain passes. The dogs were first trained back in the 1600s by monks living in the Alps.

Why do mountain houses have sloping roofs?

A sloping roof stops too much snow piling up on top of a mountain house – the extra snow slides off, like a skier sliding down a slope. The parts of the roof that stick out beyond the walls are very wide, too, to keep the falling snow away from the walls.

Why do farmers build steps on mountains?

In many parts of the world, mountain farmers build low walls to stop rainwater washing the soil away. This creates stepped fields called terraces, where the soil is deep enough for crops to grow.

- Lake Titicaca is too high for many trees to grow, so everything from boats to houses is made out of reeds.

- If you don't want to build a house on a mountain, you can always live a cave. Since earliest times, the people of Cappadocia, Turkey, have tunnelled homes in weird chimneys of volcanic rock.

Who fishes on the world's highest lake?

At 3,812 metres above sea level, Lake Titicaca in Peru, South America, is the highest navigable lake in the world. Local people live on islands in the lake and fish from boats woven from reeds.

- Some mountain rivers are blocked and turned into lakes by a strong high wall called a dam. The lake water is used to drive machines that generate electricity.

Who built palaces in the mountains?

Back in the 1400s, the Incas ruled over vast parts of the Andes Mountains of South America. They built amazing stone towns and palaces in the mountains, including the mysterious Machu Picchu.

● The Incas were conquered by Spanish invaders in the 1500s. When American explorer Hiram Bingham stumbled across Machu Picchu in 1911, it had been deserted for well over 400 years.

Which monks live in the mountains?

Mount Athos in Greece is home to 20 monasteries, and lots and lots of monks. It isn't a single peak. It is a mountainous strip of land that sticks out like a finger from the mainland.

Which city is on top of the world?

Tibet borders the Himalayas, and it's so high that people call it the 'roof of the world'. It's no surprise, then, that the Tibetan city of Lhasa is the world's highest, at 3,600 metres above sea level.

● Even valley bottoms in Tibet are higher than most countries' mountains.

● Women aren't allowed to visit Mount Athos – even female animals are banned!

Who were the mountain men?

American explorers like Kit Carson became known as mountain men during the 1800s, because they roamed through the wildest parts of the Rocky Mountains, trapping beaver and other animals for their fur.

When did the first person climb a mountain?

Although people must have been scrambling up high mountains for thousands of years, we only know about the climbers whose stories have been recorded in writing. One of the first recorded high climbs took place in AD633, when a Japanese monk called En no Shokaku made it to the top of Mount Fuji.

● One of the first rock climbers on record was a Roman soldier. In 106BC he scaled a steep cliff face hunting for rock snails to eat – and discovered a path which the rest of the army then used to make a surprise attack on an enemy camp.

Who were the first people to climb Mount Everest?

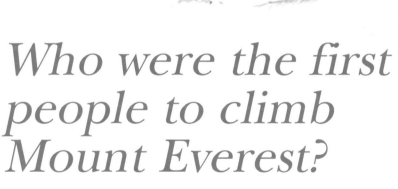

The first people to climb the world's highest mountain were Edmund Hillary of New Zealand and Tenzing Norgay of Nepal. They reached the summit of Everest on 29 May 1953.

How do people climb mountains?

Climbers use special equipment to help them get up steep rock faces, over slippery ground, and to protect them from falls. Ropes are a climber's lifeline – one end goes around the waist, and the other is looped through metal spikes called pitons, which are hammered into the rock as the climber moves upwards.

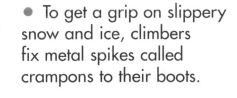

● To get a grip on slippery snow and ice, climbers fix metal spikes called crampons to their boots.

● The first woman to get to the top of Mount Everest was Junko Tabei of Japan, on 16 May 1975.

How do people surf on snow?

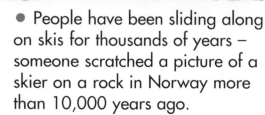

They head for the mountains with a snowboard! Snowboards are a cross between a ski, a surfboard and a wheel-less skateboard. When they were first made in the 1960s, they were called 'Snurfers'.

● People have been sliding along on skis for thousands of years – someone scratched a picture of a skier on a rock in Norway more than 10,000 years ago.

● Keen snowboarders don't give up when spring comes and the snow melts. They just switch to a new kind of souped-up skateboard – the mountainboard.

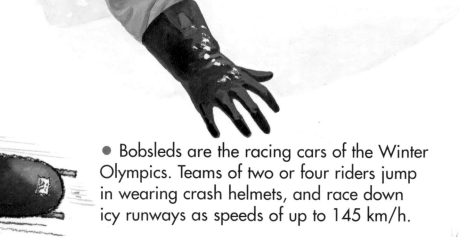

● Bobsleds are the racing cars of the Winter Olympics. Teams of two or four riders jump in wearing crash helmets, and race down icy runways as speeds of up to 145 km/h.

Who hurtles down mountains faster than an express train?

High-speed trains can zip along at over 200 km/h, and so can speed-skiers and snowboarders. Speed-skiers are the fastest – the world record is nearly 250 km/h.

Which bike climbs mountains?

A mountain bike has lots of gears to help you pedal up steep tracks, and knobbly tyres for gripping slippery slopes. And if the going gets too tough, you can always get off and carry the bike!

Which is the longest mountain tunnel?

Switzerland is home to some of Europe's highest mountains as well as to the world's longest road tunnel. The St Gotthard tunnel burrows for just over 16 kilometres through the Alps, linking Switzerland to Italy.

● Over 2,000 years ago, a general called Hannibal led an army and 40 shivering African war elephants over the Alps to attack Rome.

Where is the world's highest railway?

Passengers on the railway between Lima and Huancayo in Peru, South America, need a good head for heights. The line crosses the Andes Mountains, and the train climbs to over 4,800 metres above sea level.

● To stop them slipping backwards, the wheels on some mountain trains come in threes instead of the usual two. The third wheel is in the middle and it's toothed so it hooks on to a racked track.

Which is the steepest railway?

The view is fantastic on the Katoomba Scenic Railway in Australia's Blue Mountains, but the ride is pretty hairy. This railway is the world's steepest, dropping 415 metres in a little under two minutes.

● While you're in South America, jump on the world's longest cable car ride. It runs for about 12 kilometres up into the Andes, from the Venezuelan city of Mérida.

Where is 'the great pebble'?

The world's largest rock is a special place for the Aborigines of central Australia who call it Uluru, meaning 'great pebble'. Uluru soars nearly 348 metres above the surrounding desert, and measures nearly 9 kilometres around its base.

● Uluru glows a brilliant red when the Sun hits it at dawn and dusk. When the sky is cloudy, it looks like the back of a huge sleeping elephant.

Why do people climb Mount Fuji?

At 3,776 metres, Mount Fuji is the highest mountain in Japan and one of the world's most famous mountains. It's also one of Japan's holiest places – more than half a million people climb it every year to say their prayers on its summit.

● The ancient Greeks believed that Zeus, the king of their gods, lived in a glittering palace at the top of Mount Olympus. Olympus rises to 2,917 metres and is the highest mountain in Greece.

Which mountain looks like a table top?

Table Mountain in South Africa was named because its summit is as flat as a table top. It is often covered in clouds, which people call the Tablecloth.

● Africa's highest mountain is Kilimanjaro. At 5,895 metres, Kilimanjaro is so high that its top is always covered by snow and ice – even though it's in hot lands, close to the equator.

Index